Earth Hagiography

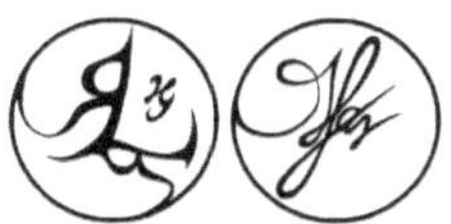

ALSO BY SFARDA L. GÜL

The Hypostasis of Dissent Duology
Non Serviam (I)
Non Omnis Moriar (II)

Feed the Forest and Never Choose Death

POETRY PUBLISHED IN:

Musing Publications
From Heart to Stomach
Mollusk Literary
Metachrosis Literary
Full House Literary
Qafiyah Review
HyeBred Magazine
Split Pomegranate
The Malu Zine

and others

SHORT STORIES PUBLISHED IN:

The Globe Review

EARTH HAGIOGRAPHY

A Poetic Florilegium

Sfarda L. Gül

CONTENT WARNINGS

Gruesome imagery.
Discussions of death.
Discussions of surgery.
Discussions of genocide, land theft, colonialism.
Discussions of mental illness, suicide, self-harm.
Discussions of oppression, police state violence.
Turkish racial slurs weaponised against indigenous minorities (*narrative purposes*).

Take care of yourself, reader; your
wellbeing comes first~♡

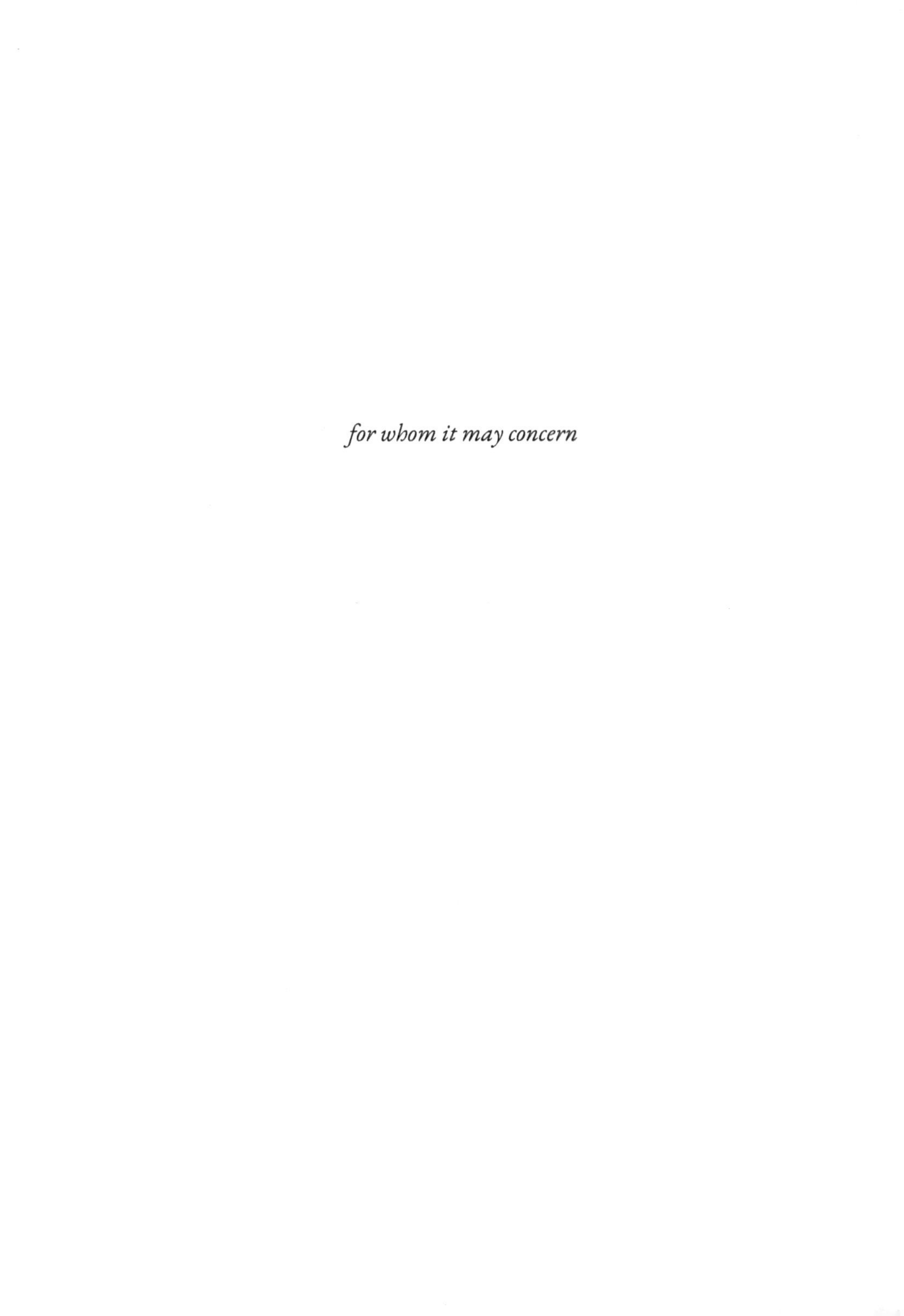

for whom it may concern

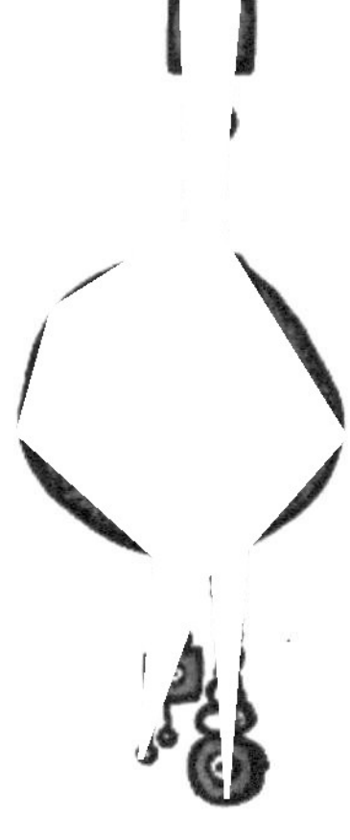

a foreword...

I *had* debated writing one of those-what the heading says—but at the last moment decided against it. My entire life I have attempted to moralise all which I do, justify it, infuse it with some definition. If you in earnest seek my lucid thoughts, I should point you to *Lacrimosity and Righteous Rage* on Substack, where I commentate as is per my wont.

Here, I will lay the cryptic verses out like antique paraphernalia for perusal and let you, reader, derive whatever meaning you glean. And you never know, perhaps you'll deduce a glimpse of me, throughout.

~Sfar

reading is political

CANTO I

Etheric Scriptures

*"I wish, God, you were a drunk
to save the whole human race."*

—Leftéris Hapsiádis

ACT OF CREATION

First published in *The Malu Zine*

Needle & thread. Untouched vestal linen.
Fingertips of diligence scribing mnemonics of

      red upon white like snow hugging rowan berries
      for warmth because one's naked back beseeches

knowledge the rusk-dry pages of history
books cannot impart & where did it go?

      Where did I put this calcified needle, this fossilised
      mortar, the petrified pestle, my teacup of toadstools?

Those flimsy pages of mortal histories
dry as rusk would burn so easily

      but I live where soil tastes like honesty so I sit sewing this
      linen with diligently bleeding fingertips & this is flesh

& veins are twisted eternity
& I am undying

TIME (NONLINEAR)

First published in *Musing Publications*

Trees of dendrites branch into

electric memories like billions
of dryad arms sprouting young

buds of today. Tomorrow, the
leaves will unfold to become

yesterday, fresh today-buds
emerging in its stead like tiny

foeti waiting to develop into
new recollections for later.

Every branch.   *Time*, young spark.
Every arm.   Time is a branching dendrite

Each its own signal.   and memories are its leaves;
Each its own time.   crackles of myelin histories.

DEW

First published in *HNDL Mag*

Roriferous and umbrose, these
alpenglow daybreaks.

Breaths

syncopate to crisp zephyr
as, beneath half-somnolent feet,

dewdrops launch for the
enubilous welkin

like

nebulised diamond dust;
ablutions of awakening.

BUTTERFLY
First published in *HNDL Mag*

did you cause that far-off storm,

revenant creature of transmutation?

CURIO_S
First published in *HNDL Mag*

Isn't it curious how necklaces tangle

without being touched—just lying

in their pouches and boxes?

GARDEN

Petals of letters blossom to words but *gods*

sometimes it grows so arduous to pick the

right stems and tie orchid-pink ribbons

around them into a pretty bouquet.

IL SOLE E LA LUNA

an excerpt from Non Omnis Moriar *by Sfarda L. Gül*

The mutilated sun bled upon the
gold-leaf sky as if a king's severed

head across a ballroom floor.
One needed to lose a lot of blood

for a surface to glisten so red.
Maybe the moon would tourniquet

the sun's wounds with her pearl
necklace so he may flash his white

teeth in gloating immortality
come tomorrow's dawn.

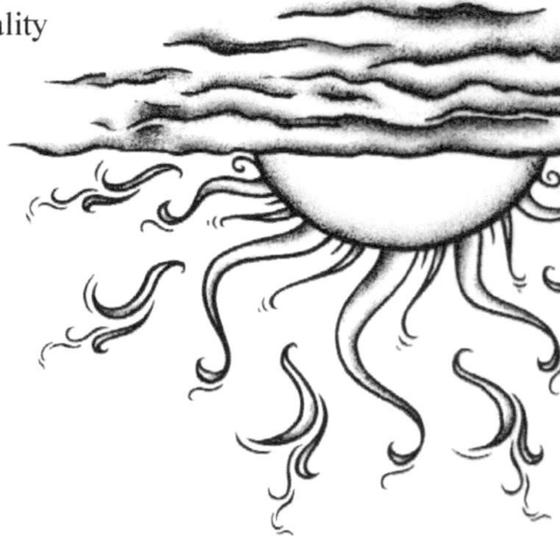

TAXIDERMY

First published in *From Heart to Stomach*

I like to think when happy
moments pass, they die,

but I wish they left
a corpse so I could

gut it and stuff it and
preserve it evermore.

ACHAMOTH

for Pístis Sophía

I saw seven dreams.

My blood birthed a black-fanged

demon for each one. It tore my wrists

to get out. Left me to rot on the sea-lapped

pebbles where the salt ate my liver

and weaved my hair into pearls.

SPEAKING HEXADECIMAL

I found her corpse in Pixie Hollow.
She opened her glaucous eyes and
told me to find the sage.

I stumbled through a dead Neverland;
under a keening waterfall. The fleshless
mermaid told me the sage met his demise

at the edge of a razorblade.
I lost my way. Bloodroot
and mandrake sprouted

in the cage of my decayed ribs.
I died beneath the birch tree which
ate my young maiden soul.

PROSELYTE

First published in *As Alive Journal*
a poetic exploration of the love of my duology's main pair (bless them, my gods)

'*you hate me*' you said with those eyes
etched from quartz, '*hate me more*'.

you spoke eighteen languages, one for each of
the grey hairs sprung up among my ringlets,

given birth by the throes of my plight your
bladed nails imprinted indelibly upon my

tapestry. My eyes threw daggers and I caught
them, drove their copper razors into your

arteries woven of stars and madness.
So I could drink them. So I was madness.

I was a star to burn the fire that were you.
'*I hate you*'. You asked me to tell you '*why*'.

I broke your quartz eyes, took each shard to
lodge into my corneas. I wanted to see what

you saw. You knew too much and they hated you.
I hated you. *'why?'* I was wrath and you

were hubris. I was bloodlust and you were
eleutheromania. I was *katō Sophia* and

you were an atheist. Two-fold heresy. *'why, because*
you are me, because I made your eyes my flesh,

eyes that were not quartz, eyes that were glass and
gnosis. *because I drank your arteries.'*

I was madness, recall? Did you intend on it when you
asked *'hate me more'*?

It nourished you. For, recall, too, you were fire.
Your starlight blood made me luminous

waters suspending the cosmos. But you,
I burned not. Deluge, me. Never *you*, me.

I hated you. And you
believed in a deity.

SOMETHING VERY GENTLE

First published in *As Alive Journal*

You pretend the slamming door is thunder—
not human wrath but *Earth's*; justified.

    The coldness of hands white as snow; deified.
    Screams become doves' warbles; syllabified.

Finding a razor in your bed sheets,
you cut myrtles from the dilapidated
dooryard to land yourself beneath the
blade of a guillotine instead—untried.

    To be a tender thing on tenterhooks, overwrought
    and squirrely; grasping in trembling fingers

Ares' spear and shield, harrows a soul unfit
for slaughter not because of weakness but
unimaginable strength—you'd rather
kill yourself than kill another—so

you lay down the murder tools and take up
Aphrodite's polished-copper mirror

not of choice but of that same soul's calling.
Demand. Correctness. Completeness.
Gentle as knives against the chest and a white
swan pecking out your blue eyes and pink guts

because damnation is fine if skin turns to cosmic
mnemonics of Self; ascended and stellified.

HIRAETH

an excerpt from Non Serviam *by Sfarda L. Gül*

I missed the roses I'd press between pages of old philosophy books scrawled by slated madmen, anthocyanins staining the faded beige insomnia like lipstick prints, Death preserved. I missed *The Crescent*'s pantomimes—carved from eyelids never baptised by tears of anything but pain, never permitted to. Perhaps I missed the old thespians, those faces rendered in distorted oil paint like tongues held by scissor-blade silence.

I did not miss that theatre—that frozen, hollow skull. I did not miss an upper world baying for my blood. My mind.

Once, I misshaped myself to fit the mould of a realm I held no place in out of fear, knowing Otherness meant Death.

Now, finally, I saw the universe tending towards entropy, unfurling both without and within like tempestuous waters, rebirthing my Shadow.

Blindness in pure light...

This lucifugous world, the heartbeat of caliginous darkness inside its flesh, was... *totality*. My duality beginning to seal shut.

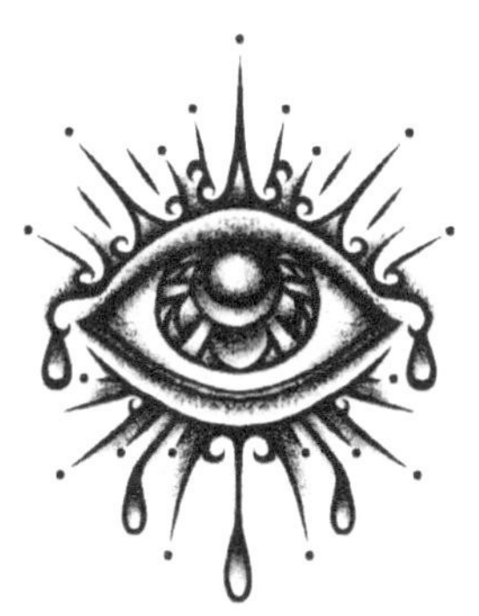

Shadows speak truth.

CANTO II

Documenting Ruination

*"In order for me to write poetry that
isn't political, I must listen to the birds,
and in order to hear the birds, the
warplanes must be silent."*

—Marwān Makhūl

WHEN I OPENED MY EYES,

the solid soil had submerged like

Atlantis beneath the tears of icecaps
and *oh* was it a tragicomic

scene to see the waters burn with

black oil slick as obsidian and watch
the carbon sky blister with napalm.

First published in *Metachrosis Literary*

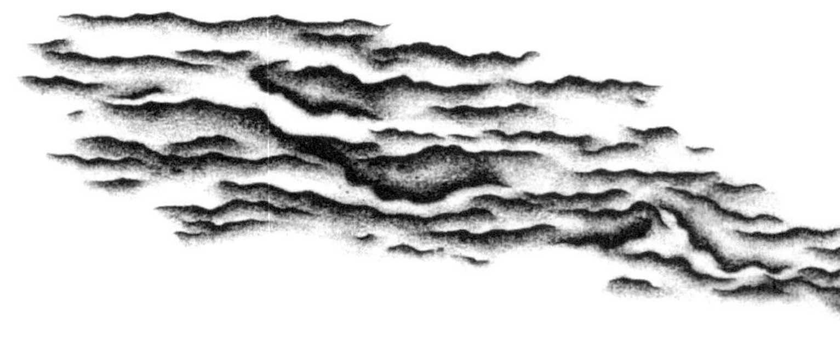

ADDICTIVE PERSONALITY

Dead hair on the bathroom wall.
I'll take it none or all at once.

NATURELESS SPHERICITY

First published in *Metachrosis Literary*

Above Earth you fancy yourself

        Untouchable

A stone dagger

A deranged creature

    Vinaceous flesh ichor teeth

Unkillable killer

Civilised barbarian in green plastic cotton paper

        Blood money

Blood of Earth you fancy yourself above of

You will not kneel beneath the thumb of time?

But Babylon fell

Mişr burned

    Sumer crumbled

    Erlik wept

All mouldens in the Earth

        yet you forget the mother of

your stone dagger whose womb bleeds

like your teeth against the vinaceous squelch of flesh

you deranged creature

and Nature isn't real!

Oh! Civilised barbarian a dichotomy

you construct in false pretence

                              above
              to ascend   Earth

but heed the screams of Babylon and

Alexandria and Ur and Karakorum:

        All mouldens

                in this Natureless sphericity;

        Your blood money will buy you rot

I FOUND A QUARTER

Fifteen and eighty-one and a dead man

but how much can I stomach of an atomic bomb

                     under my tongue? Incompatible

                          impending doom

   like group two

      against

       group three—

       the world choking

     on grume and shaking in fever

     before death and why haven't

I slit open my tongue with

    rusty Hiroshima shrapnel (?)

I want these words taken from me

  despite my pride in them.

             Undeserving so freeze them in nuclear winter.

I detest this plane;

       euclidea repels me.

A quarter is not enough to pay my rent for

                        eighty-one years

              until I lie a dead man

       beneath fifteen mounds

of clotted dirt under an atomic sky I threw up

           so let my fever abate you brute!

You cursed euclidea

     you blasted impending doom

you throat-slitter

       maniacal white atom bomb, suicide pill, SSRI,

       melatonin, IV drip, a quarter for my rent,

a detestable plane, a tongue, a shrapnel,

fever, doom.

SPRING'S DIRGE (*English*)

It is already spring.

     Apricot, pomegranate, wild cherry.

Free of charge!

   A gift of Earth.

    Do you still hope?

   Sometimes, I feel like a motherless child.

        Why?

It is already spring!

      Bone, scab, blood.

    Free of charge?

Nowhere in the world!

  The Earth is dead.

ΜΟΙΡΟΛΌΓΕΜΑΝ ΤΗΣ ΆΝΟΙΞΗΣ

(pseudo-Pontic)

Είναι κιόλας άνοιξη.
Íne kiólas ánixi.

Ζέρταλο, νάριν, αγροκέρασον.
Zértalo, nárin, aḡrokérason.

Τζάμπα!
Tzába!

Ένα αρμαγάς της Γης.
Éna armaḡás tis Υis.

Ακόμα ελπίζεις;
Akóma elpízis?

Καγκαμμίαν, νιώθω σαν γαρδέλη χωρίς μητέρα.
Kankammían, niótho san ḡardéli horís mitéra.

Ογιά;
Oγiá?

Είναι κιόλας άνοιξη.
Íne kiólas ánixi.

Στούδιν, μαυροτέγανο, γαίμα.
Stoúḍin, mavrotéḡano, γíma.

Τζάμπα;
Tzába?

Ουδαμού του ντουνιά!
Ouḍamoú tou douniá!

Η Γη είναι αψυχωμένη.
I Υi íne apsyhoméni.

SOLASTALGIA

I think we're lost in:

> 9. an ash forest;

> 8. a firestorm at sea;

> 7. a hydrogen sulphide heaven;

> 6. a nucl_ar winter;

blistering;

> parched;

unliveable

and c_rpse-littered as:

> 5. cherry blossoms *gone extinct beneath a*:

> 4. fishnet ozone;

but at least the dr_g w_rs

were funded with:

> 3. bloody US dollars,

> > so—

the skyglow of apoc_lypse

> can dance a:

> 2. kaleidoscopic *kótsari*

and the g_noc_dal wh_te sun

can glow like *galgalim* urging:

> 1. *'do not fear.'*

Too late—

I unlearned such luxuries

when we got lost.

First published in *Full House Literary*
under the title *I Think We're Lost*

BURNOUT

a collapse flagrates inside me / I will estuate and
detonate / erupt / I will misfire like
a gun and burn out

VANITY

bone-thin dignity measurable in notches;
calories and skeletal protrusions.

what *vanity* when such suffering presides;
eaten alive by a famished body of self?

ARTIFICIAL LIFE

In my skin lingers the taste of surgical thread
and syringe; remnants of humming cold light;
sterile wall in my milk teeth;
scalpel tongue (*I love it*).
Cardiopulmonary bypass whining–
–machine heartbeat.
I think I died
on that surgery table,
autopsy table,
and walked a dead bitch
for [*going on*] 16 years.
Rip the catheter from my throat, bleed
on the bed of that ugly cardiac ward:
I nearly tore out of myself when
I smelled it again at age 13—
zombified Frankenstein's doll.
(reanimated)

Stagnant blood a pill cocktail
dialysis couldn't cleanse.

I like throwing up acid

                    on the marble floors

                    of politicians–

     –making room for that glazed hide

     of theirs, my hors d'oeuvre.

    Dead bitch; nothing to lose.

    Dead bitch; your Frankenstein children's

                    zombified doll.

    Those little silver-spoon shits

          you sent to school

        to study the art of

      vivisection and

    haberdashery

        on flesh–

            –the ones who gave me

              my machine heart

   and an extra couple decades of living

on this throat-strangler plastic planet.

Dead bitch;
        artificial life;
                        I *f* a
                           1 *l*

        a / p / a / r / t

                                at
                              ʌɯ
                                s:e:a:
                                m:s;

        my blood oozes

                into nurses' vacuum tubes

                                (*not spouts*);

                my milk teeth

        turn to powder

in an empty old jewellery box

        (*still crusted with sterile wall like crowns*).

        Humming cold light

        in my dead bitch eyes.

                        (reanimated)

My scalpel tongue

        loves to cut, too.

MOMMY ISSUES

One thing I will be to men is their worst nightmare.
Cthulhu in a white summer dress—

mind-shatterer.

Your mommy was mean? Mine dug me from
the earth to chew on my marrow
and spit me into a ditch,

now I bite jugulars.

And today my gums itch.

EXTERMINATING SELF

One step, *two* step.
Plan, method, [*self-*]execution.
I flew with the angels thrice and came plummeting
—rejected like incompatible grafts. *Festered.*

DSBM on repeat as the bleak sky-flesh flakes, mine
counting the ceiling cracks, *roach tracks.* Lying on
my back makes a hollow of my gut; skin stretched
over worker's washboard ribs; tree hollow cage
birthing Yárilo The Summer-Maker.

Laughing through the itch of cut-up thighs, I smear the
crimson canyons with myrrh, dabbing leaks away with
prósphoron like the last beetroot soup of desolate northern
winter where grey floorboards creak and blizzards wail.
Where fox blood tinges the murderous air. Where nooses
hang hungry as our ghosts and razor blades.

I laugh until the frost rakes my lungs
and my wrists thaw the winter.

Plan, method, [*self-*]execution.

Razor, fox, rib.
Final step.

I hang in limbo sempiternally—
cannot cut myself free to plummet
into oblivion; *tetramorph*.

I sew to me a piece of flaked sky.
I bite the fox's liver.
I lay the prósphoron for the noose to eat
and release from my flesh of the
incompatible meat.

But I don't fly with the angels still
—the throat-strangler plastic planet
demands my steps haunt it evermore.

So I laugh through the cut-up itch and
squash that roach Yárilo under my thumb.

I'll stay wailing
with the blizzards here.

ROTTEN

Like medlar—

only good when dying.

CANNIBALOVE

First published in *From Heart to Stomach*

I love you the way flesh loves its skin

PALMFUL

First published in *From Heart to Stomach*

Your words are a palmful of
pills I swallow for my pain.

I'd rather not overdose a 3rd time but I
detest anaemic nights and unsharpened

razor blades so maybe your
smoke-and-bubblegum voice

is okay to take on a bulimic stomach
(*I promise I'm trying like you pleaded*).

INTIMACY

a strangle Val Day ramble I do not understand either

thoughts bleed out in words

like

a strawberry

beneath the pressure of hands,

of fingers,

scratched fingers like scratched tiles,

lost acrylics,

broken nails,

nails in skin

to write signatures by

scratched fingers

curled in time with hair and Zippo flame.

Zippo flame

to wax as breath to frost.

amorphous ephemera.

corset lace and sapphic rouge

surpassed by raw imprints of boning

upon soft flesh and

flushed cheeks the colour

of strawberry juice

and smeared lipgloss,

smudged kohl,

liquor tongue, red light green light Nine Inch Nails

My Chemical Romance

purple haze

cigarette stench

black hair

black fishnet

silver chain

silver giggle.

silly words play pretend

as if graffiti of anarchy

doesn't tattoo these pasty walls

wrapped in tattered posters; streaked in grime

and sweaty cxcaine handprints

but an amorphous ephemera

leaves behind benevolent bruises.

LAMIA'S SPECIMEN

First published in *From Heart to Stomach*

Love is a scalpel and circumstances are the

dissection table upon which she becomes

a crippled specimen for you.

Beating heart for you,

     quivering lungs for you,

   pulsing veins,

        wine-sweet blood and meaty marrow

           for *you*.

   Drink her.

   Feast upon her.

Slice her angelite lips from my pearl teeth

to purify her. Unzip her skin

     off her carcass and

unspool her ailing brain in which resides

            only *you*

    because without you she's nothing so

    here she is, drained and eviscerated

    on your dissection table,

her organs in your glass

jars and eyeballs dangling from

your ears like jewellery.

You said her eyes look like covellines.

She doesn't know what that is

but she knows it's blue

like her dumb

and dead

lips.

Maybe that's why you wore her

like gemstone adornments.

Maybe we'll only ever be pretty

dismembered by you

but she doesn't mind

because you look gorgeous

as fresh suicide

in blue

and she's

too *dumb and dead*, so, love,

she'll be a specimen for you.

ASPHALT DREAMS (*English*)

And why is it, when I sense

the scent of factories,

I,

in my thrall,

recall a forgotten

childhood?

And when mica glistens on the asphalt

of this Hellish foundation,

I am visited by

the sensation of blind delight

(?)

Beat-up porches;

gnarled playgrounds;

a hernia in the antrum of the world.

And I—ill

terminally.

АСФАЛЬТНЫЕ МЕЧТЫ (*Russian*)

И почему когда
I pochemú kogdá

я чую запах заводов,
ya chúyu zápah zavódov,

Я,
ya,

во своей пленносте,
vo svoyéy plénnoste,

вспоминаю забытое
vspomináyu zabıtoye

детство?
détstvo?

И когда слюда блестит на асфальте
I kogdá slyudá blestít na asfál'te

этого Адского фундамента, меня
ǝtovo Ádskovo fundámenta, menyá

посещает чувство
poseshcháyet chúvstvo

слепого восторга
slepóvo vostórga

(?)

Побитые подъезды;
Pobobítıye pod''yézdı;

сгнитые площадки;
sgnítıye ploshchádki;

грыжа в животе мира.
grızha v zhivoté míra.

И я—больна
I ya—bol'ná

пожизненно.
pozhíznenno.

TORIES AND TANKIES // Ⓐ

Reds-Blues

lick oppressor boot,

just different shit.

Dogma's your cxcaine

—tongues too numb

to the taste of leather

to realise it.

(P) ꙅ(A) ꙅ(I) ꙅ(N)

First published in *Split Pomegranate*

I return to you my ability to feel pain.

I don't need it beneath this seething

red welt of a sun God lanced off his ankle

like a shackle to give to his children.

WE'RE NOT ALONE

but what can ghosts do

in a bitumen forest of walking corpses?
Their deaf ears are severed stumps spitting pus like
their mouths spit bile on blood thinned to
isopropanol—not water.

So what's left for our useless pleas to fall on
but asphalt of 40-years-cracked
beneath pogrom feet?

Can they see my daisy-white
and forget-me-not-blue
with glaucomatous eyes?

Red isn't poppies or apples anymore;
the ceruse winter sky tastes of ashes here too.

BLOODY BUTTERCUPS

Buttercups bloom between cobbled paths of your
timeworn house, petals like burnished coins—

the cost of a life left unlived.
Buttercups you pick to twirl

between feeble fingertips.

To eat their poison petals
so they might sprout in your
core where you'd grown so empty.

The colour of joy but joy is dead like
worms frozen beneath frore skins

of winter-throttled earth.
Buttercups with their sour petals like blood.

You never thought blood might taste like this.

Blood tastes like regret, every mealy-mouthed
confession never plucked from the throat.

Blood tastes like loss. Like worms and winter.

Blood tastes like a life

                      left unlived.

Canto III

Winds of the

Mountains; Black

Ichor of the Sea; Algid

Dead North

"I don't know who sold our homeland,
but I saw who paid the price."

—Maḥmūd Darwīsh

CHILD AND OUTCAST

First published in *HyeBred Magazine*

I—

belonging nowhere.

on every land

both child and

outcast.

BLOODLINE

First published in *HyeBred Magazine*

Peace, when

(?)

My headscarf

is frayed at

the edges of my

bloodline.

RECALL

First published in *Mollusk Literary*

Maúron Thálassa. Uça Zuǧa.
Kiršnas Mári. Sew Dzov.
K(G)araden(ň)iz.

        Did I recall correctly?

My *máti* stares at me from a needle pinning to my wall

the map of a land my feet are yet to tread upon,

warding off envious blue-eyed glares.

Yet my feet recall that soil from

immemorial centuries gone by

when sycamore and lime scattered

the grassland of that old plateau

and *Vits'e* smelled of *pakhlava,*

lokum, paponi.

Halvás tastes of childhood.
From حلوا (*halvâ*), if I recall.

Only sunflower—the kind my
northern siblings favour.

My ancestors' Anatolian tongue
craves the sesame of fasting on

Sarakostí. The semolina of
returning from *Ḥajj* and the

peanut of escape to Argentina
from the Ottoman sword.

My *máti* stares,
asking me, '*do you recall?*'

PANIHÍDA

We killed ourselves in the rye fields.
You and I adored the hoarfrost light
of November misery.

You were misery. You
hooked rusty metal hinges to
the ridges of my plagued brain.

The white Sunday church bells sang
a liturgy in Old Church Slavonic that day.
The language we cut our hands on to make

our own—a language with hungry teeth.
You told me to recite my scriptures. But
it was Marena I gave my wintry prayer to.

No, mother. It was not *my* language. It was
yours—those cannibals
made you believe so.

Novgorod's bones are parched as birch bark.

I spoke the language of the meadows the holy
men stomped. The forests where we carved
our sun of scythes. The river who listened

to our laments before the red-robed reapers cut our
monuments away. '*The devil came out of the
gnarled wood*,' they blazoned.

Moscovia ate our roots.
And you were me.

So I killed myself in the rye fields.

Only you.

Only me.

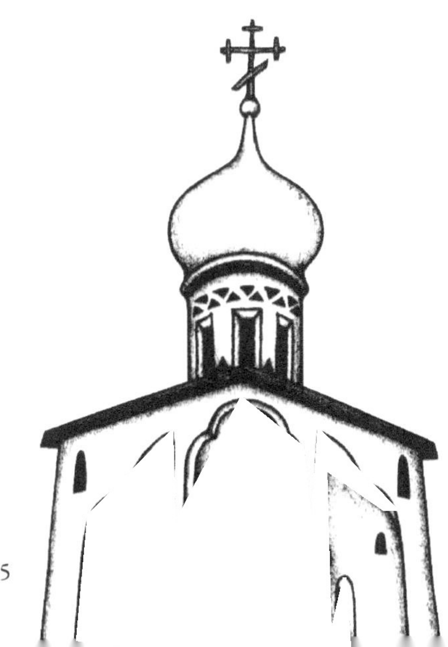

A CURSE UPON YOUR
BLOODLINE, DESECRATOR

Your footprints moulden
in the soil you senselessly tread.

In the pocket of my Ural-black
sarafán sleeps a roll of thread
scarlet as my ancient blood.

Blood not of *you*. Blood of *me*.
Us and earth—*this soil
you senselessly tread.*

I lay, unrolled, the thread upon
your passage's putrescent vestige;
measure your sententiousness.

My scissors scream SNIP—slice
in twain the thread like a
flailing pit viper; bleeding.

Bleeding like me and this
Ural soil—desecrated.
Unknown, forgotten, keening.

Gods, why won't you listen?
Gods, why won't you unmake?
Gods. Gods. "*God_* ," you said.

The measure of your sententiousness.
I put the thread to the pyre, uttering a
curse upon your bloodline, desecrator!

PURGATORY (*it's under the floorboards*)

You'll only see the colour of my
mother's eyes in my own when
sunlight illuminates their curvature.

(she calls her hazel eyes "swamp-coloured")

There *is* no sun in the north where my maternal
branches are rooted. Only dark glimmers
leaking like lard between the wooden
floorboards of a decaying grey house.

(my maternal soil is a Balto-Slavic mutt)

My neighbour asks me why Hittite cuneiform is
etched into my arms (*my paternal ancestors
were Hellenised Anatolians*); I tell him
northerners like the pain of
splinters and rope.

*(some say Russians have never known freedom
so slavery is their comfort)*

He doesn't realise we are trapped

between a dead Novgorod and

a cannibalistic Moscovia.

(she was the one who ate him with

Kyiv's help, then she ate Kyiv)

REPOSSESSION

Once you give something a name,
you give it power.
        But,
once you give something a name,
you can control it.
      Profile it.
      Chain it.
      Banish it.

On his Soviet documents, my paternal
grandfather's name was "Лазарь" (*Lázar'*).
But that wasn't his name.
See, my paternal ancestors were gold-black
bees fleeing from the locust swarms, finding
themselves in the nest of scarlet fire ants.

      What I'm trying to say is their choice
      was between Orwell's nightmare
      and Deir ez-Zūr.

From one empire to another, both a bloodthirsty demon.
Both a reaper and a conferrer of names.

Do you see why "Lázar'" *wasn't* my
paternal grandfather's name?

It was Λάζαρος (*Lázaros*).
From Ἐλεάζαρ (*Eleázar*).
From אֶלְעָזָר (*'Eli'azár*).
"My God has helped".

But had He?

Locusts devoured half of the beehive,
and time slipped away like blood
down the mountainside.

Do you recall when it was

Կարին (*Karin*), not "Erzurum"?

Does the memory jog when you hear

Τραπεζούντα (*Trapezoúnta*) or ტამტრა

(*T'amt'ra*) in place of "Trabzon"?

Or ܥܝܢܘܪܕܐ (*Ayin Wardo*), not "Gülgöze"?

Did you know it was Θεοδοσία (*Theodosía*),

not "Феодóсія" (*Feodósia*)?

Did you know he was *Hovhannes Aivazian*?

Did you know

he was Armenian?

And it's not "America", is it?

Neither was it "Kiev".

Neither was it "Şuşa".

Even "Çamlıhemşin". A bone thrown

to the slaughtered settlers—Homshetsis

never lived in Pontos until migrating

from Western Armenia, you know.

It's „ვიჯა" (*Vija*).

It's Laz.

Where my maternal family comes from,

there's an empty patch in the forest.

The old slave-owner's house once stood there.

Every summer, my uncle (mother's
brother) and his friends go there to make
shashlyk and bum around like an ironic
dig at the long-gone serfdom days.
I love irony.

Where my maternal family comes from,
there's a slur for what we are:
Дереве́нщина (*derevénshchina*).

A "villager". A rustic. A commoner. A yokel.
Dehumanising. Derogatory.
I love irony, but it hurts, sometimes.

Upon your very own land, to your very own
compatriots: lowborn filth, all because your
title—*name*—isn't "Muscovite".
But such is the nature of Orwell's nightmare.

See, it *was* "Lázaros": past tense.
But "Lázaros" got one profiled and banished by the
scarlet fire ants for "Otherness" (such was the
nature of Orwell's nightmare, after all).

"Lázar'" granted power—*the power to*
skirt profiling and banishment
—but it chained.

When the Ottomans swarmed, surviving
indigenous Pontians fled to Russia, a land
first a bloodsoaked plantation ruled by fat
silkworms, then USSR's Queen Ant.
Always scarlet.

From one empire to another.

I find it funny, in a profoundly saddening way, that Orwell's
nightmare—a nest of scarlet ants who burned boundless fields
no worse than the locusts devoured the mountains, who kept
green butterfly wings studded with golden stars as trophies
and crawled east to raze the homes of soft-hearted moths
—was the one to take pity on those fugitive bees.
Where would they go if the anthill banished them too?

If you plug your ears
from the Soviet anthem,
it sounds like an SS march.

I love irony, but it hurts.

All of this hurts—to be a child of Orwell's
nightmare and devoured Anatolia both.

Once you give something a name,

you can control it.

It?

The narrative, hun.

That's why they won't say

"totalitarianism".

That's why they won't say

"colonisation".

That's why they won't say

"genocide".

There are gentler names to be conferred:

It's *"propaganda"*.

It's *"a union"*.

It's *"myth"*.

To name it all correctly is

to allow for repossession

by the original owner, but

the reaper seeks dominion.

NOT EVEN MY NAME

after Thea Halo

When the mountains fell, they devoured
our kin, like great big masticators grinding
meat to mince, veins its drink, fat pooling
in the karst cracks to warm cliffs
through the Ottoman winter.

The razed earth begged for all the nourishment in the world
    and what suits better than your own flesh and blood?
(Mama rabbits eat their progeny in desperation, after all).

    When the mountains fell, our shredded bones lodged
like splinters into the bloated skin of the earth—everywhere
but the razed flesh from which we sprouted like hairs, black
as the Sea, as our eyes, as charred hides.

My paternal bloodline lodged into the North, an
ugly, thrawn snaggletooth of God's grief for
Constantinopolis, a sharp cuneiform prong, a
transplanted organ rejected by the new body.

Cold white faces stalked in a ghostly procession
the moaning blizzards of those serfdom streets,
dragging their gangrenous feet nowhere.

There *were* no mountains there, just a polar desert.
A frozen Deir ez-Zūr along which Old Novgorod
hauled his half-cannibalised husk like a zombie
ripped from the hoarfrost earth and restless.

(He doesn't beg to live, anymore).

My mother grew up in the USSR.
Her mother grew up in the USSR.
    Her mother stood witness
to the USSR's birth.

The USSR was Moscovia's child; the USSR broke
bones and drank marrow—every inch its mother's
bastard. But not the way the mountains did.

Moscovia glutted on all which pulsed the way

a wretched man drinks himself into oblivion,

the way a Western king gobbles down a feast.

Moscovia ate Novgorod and took his

home, once a communal dwelling of

Balts, Slavs, Finns.

Moscovia clawed at the belly of

the Ottomans, the Ottomans who

fell our mountains, but it didn't

save her from becoming them.

(You are what you eat, they say).

The USSR, *every inch its mother's bastard*, ripped

away the last of poor Novgorod's old skin when it

learned to walk and hold—Novgorodian Slavs were

banished beneath the poverty line, too far from

Moscow, Novgorodian Balts and Finns were banished

east to the Siberian death camps, stolen land.

The USSR vivisected the scarred

Armenian body, "gifting" a slice of

her pulsing meat to Azeris to eat.

For Stalin to get in good with Atatürk.

Every inch its mother's fucking bastard!

Not the mountains.

When the mountains fell, they soaked our
marrow into their soil diligently between the bump
and ridge of karst, wasting not a drop, and they
wept streams for our splintered bones.

Moscovia and her child begged for dominion
and Kyiv's glory (*USSR's father was just as
much a gluttonous cannibal, now he wears
Novgorod's jewellery and claims it his*).

The mountains begged for nourishment.

The mountains begged to live.

ECHOES IN THE DESERT

First published in *Split Pomegranate*

Pomegranate arils, or the bloody

teeth of my ancestors and kith

scattered across Deir ez-Zūr?

1: WHO REMEMBERS THE ASSYRIANS?

after *Who Remembers the Armenians?* by Najwan Darwish
and *Who Remembers the Palestinians?* by Sophia Armen

I do

and I would piece Antioch, flinder by

crumbled flinder, with them each day

until the city is back together again.

And my black tea, this morning

I am drinking it with them.

You, coloniser—

Who remembers *you*?

2: WHO REMEMBERS THE LAZIS?

after *Who Remembers the Armenians?* by Najwan Darwish
and *Who Remembers the Palestinians?* by Sophia Armen

I could never forget

and I, in spirit, walk the Black Sea

coasts of Artviniş, Rizini, T'amt'ra,

with them each day.

And this mountain water, this morning

I am drinking it with them.

You, revisionist—

Who remembers *you*?

3: WHO REMEMBERS THE ANATOLIAN GREEK-SPEAKERS?

after *Who Remembers the Armenians?* by Najwan Darwish
and *Who Remembers the Palestinians?* by Sophia Armen

I always will

and I would march into Constantinopolis each

day, with a soaked cloth, until its streets are

washed clean of their bloodstains.

And my *kafés*, this morning

I am drinking it with them.

You, exiler—

Who remembers *you*?

KNOWING TOO MUCH

Everything I Know shoves my head
beneath the water and tells me
to recite it back.

Crosses marr the doors of Armenian homes
in Baku (*Bakurakert?*) and Anatolian Greek-
Speaker homes in Constantinopolis ("*İstanbul*").
The locusts will come to devour you
soon so you better run into the Sea.

You've kept breathing this long
on that razed land which birthed you.
Most of us didn't. *I* didn't (*I was born in exile—*
in the fire ant nest in the north where starved
hordes still scrub burnt lard of old kings off
floorboards bashed by NKVD boots).

Now, most of us
run into the Sea.

When Greek-speaking Anatolians washed up on
the shores of Elláda, the Hellenes called them
«Λαζοί» (*Lazí*). "Laz". And maybe they
weren't wrong, but they didn't say it like
that. Like a fact. They said it like a fault,
like a hex, like *"Asiatic mutts unworthy*
of the sacred 'Greek' nomen!"

I learn Greek because I cannot learn Pontic
(*there is nothing left*), and I catch each time
the ancient words are polished with
Romance and Germanic whetstones.

Its sharpness nicks my tongue in reminder that
it's fumbling with words not of its patrída.

I want the bones of my patrída back, I repeat, yet I
speak of goodbyes with «αντίο» (*adío*). Like *"addio"*.

No one speaks of the murdered Lazis, the ones who'd
called themselves Greeks for millennia and whose
stolen breaths toss about the bone-sands of central
Turkish deserts. And I'm the only one speaking.

My father was a proud Greek with not a
drop of Hellenic blood running through
him. But he didn't even know of Lazis.

I know of Lazis.
And I know of Homshetsis.
And Everything I Know
shoves my head beneath
the water and tells me
to recite it back.

I don't know "goodbye" in Lazuri.
I don't know "goodbye" in Homshetsi.
I don't know "goodbye" in Pontic.

So I open my mouth and breathe.

The water is Black.

The water is Sea—the one we ran into.

The water inflates my lungs, trickles

between my distended ribs.

Knowing too much suffocates but

I cannot force myself to raise my head.

I cannot force myself to stop breathing.

I cannot recite back Everything I Know.

(*I am drowning in it*)

ŞEHÎD NAMIRIN (MARTYRS NEVER DIE)

in memory of Halabja Kurds

White for peace; a dove's soft wings.
Green for the lush verdure of sparkling plains.
Red for blood of martyrs;
dignified free hearts; warriors.
Dazzling sun, twenty-one rays, gold
and hallowed as life and Newroz.

A noxious yellow-black throttled the
White of that March day; doves
dropped from the sky—*corpses*.
Green spewed from panicked lips,
choking throats, tarnished with
the Red of massacre—*corpses*.
The dazzling gold sun snuffed out
like bonfires, extinguished in eyes
never to see the pyres of sacred
scarlet Wednesday next Newroz—
only five days away—*corpses*.

Five thousand corpses.

Gold transmuted to artillery steel

                    that March day.

The verdure reeked

of apples and rotten garbage

                    that March day.

Chemical Ali's genocidal toys
made martyrs of children

                    that March day.

"It was total annihilation," a blameless
man recalled[†] the massacre of

                    that March day.

I never stood there.

In all my luck, never needed to.

But screams echo

without memory.

Without time.

Without witness.

Only razed history.

Only broken not-rhyme.

[†] *Kherwan, a Halabja native, recounted his memories of the March 16th, 1988, chemical attack against Halabja, Irāqi Kurdistan.*

WE DIED FOR THE WINDS
OF THE MOUNTAINS

after Lena Chamamyan
First published in *Qafiyah Review*

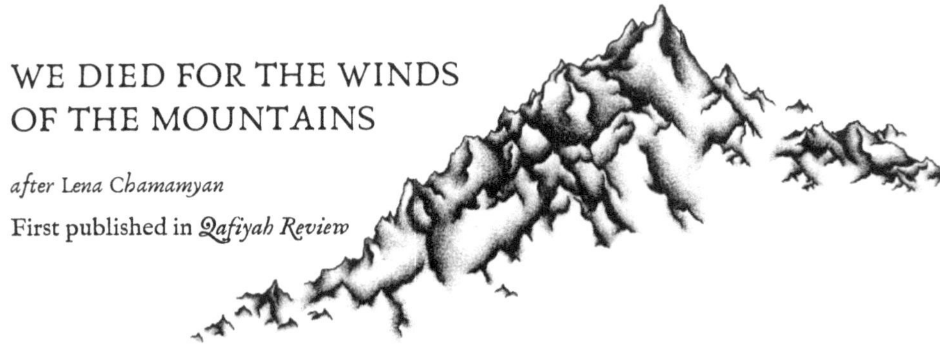

Under the Parhar I lie /

a miscarriage / an afterbirth.

I should like my tears to plenish its rivers /

my blood to nourish its soil / my lungs to feed its

winds—these membranes wrapping the swaying

grass blades and cradling the moon.

Yet blood pulses in my flesh-veins cerise

as juice / bitter like disownment.

Blood has nourished this soil too many times.

Whose?

I never did find neither my father

nor God, so I scratch at the cross and

I scratch at the masjid door but I don't know

and I don't know *I do not know*

what I am when my spongy white marrow
unspools from its callused red skin.

I am a gutted pomegranate
I try to piece together again
/ reform into a cohesive
whole it never once was.

My blood is on my own hands
cerise as juice / and why?

And who?
Where from?
Where to?

I cannot be me until I eat myself aril by bitter aril
/ until I am soil / until I am wind.

I cannot be me until I am not /
until I am under the Parhar.

MINCED WORDS

headscarf and heartbreak; heavy teeth; hawthorn
within [a] hazel grove; dead language.

A TESTAMENT TO THE
LOVE OF NOWHERE

First published in *Musing Publications*

eighth December day;

    I am Good /*proud and pure*

and filthy: a flea in fire!

a little winter cherry or quicklime

scythe-smile;

    filthy corpse country;

    yesterday—rain;

    tomorrow—war.

BORDERS

Draw a line in the sand.
Will you find it tomorrow? On this jagged
road parting a mountain the hare scales?

Have you asked the hare
what he thinks of your line?
Have you asked for the hare's name?

You would turn over every shrapnel
of karst and inscribe a moniker upon it.
Don't you know karst is sedimentary?
It breaks to smaller segments like
etymology the longer you fiddle.

That's why you take hunks out of the mountain for
yourself, drawing borders to circumscribe arbitrary
territory like salt circles but it's *saltpetre* you'll
detonate if we step too far out of line.
Karst is an unwieldy canvas for linework.

That's why you drew your line in the *sand*.

Will you find it in a week?

Will the ant cease in his tracks,

drop the pile of elytra he hauls as if gemstones,

and abide by the law of your border? Have you

ever wondered who the lawmaker is? Have you

ever heard his voice echo strained and

transitory between Andromeda

and Hoag's Object?

Small thing; silly thing.

That line of yours, the one in the sand, sprouts

flowers from the verdure coiled in its pit like a viper.

                                      It angers you, I know.

How can you name

a thing severed in twain?

Does the separation not make One a pair?

But is it not still One?

And, if so, who holds ownership

of its singularity?

Those flowers grow on either side

of the border, almost as if its line

was rendered arbitrarily.

Will you find it in a month?

   When the rains trudge through?

   When that verdure rots to nourishment

   for soil and worm?

   When hoarfrost rimes the nameless karst?

                     Earth erased your line long ago.

Don't you understand yet?

   You insist on your lines. Your borders.

   Those simplified scribbles with which you

   deface Earth's wrinkled countenance—

   the cheekbones of Her mountains

   and nose bridge of Her cliffs, the

   forests linked and sprawling

   like Her lush brows.

I remember that winter

   when a wire fence crested the mountain's ridge.

                 That became the "border".

There was a village, too.

Soon, the fence crawled closer, growing like a web,

its threads woven by spider-dark soldiers.

Soon, the village stood on the *other*
side, circumscribed, renamed—the new
moniker pierces my tongue like shrapnel of
detonated karst as it tries to wrap
around uncharted etymology.

The sky was blue as Andromeda that day.
Andromeda has another name too:

Messier 31.

You couldn't name a thing severed in twain
so you took the entire hunk for yourself.
That's how you decreed its singularity's
owner. *That's* how you seized
the unwieldy karst.

I stood on that jagged road parting
the mountain and watched you scale
lower with your spiderling colony.

The hare hopped away in the autumn rains,
the pit viper shed its scales as a parting gift,
and I never knew spiders ate ants.

Where is the line in the sand?

Have you not defaced Earth enough?
Do the valleys and canyons of Her
ancient face not suffice without scribbles?
Must all be named? What does a line
on a map mean when you don't want it
there? When you want the entire mountain,
unscalable karst and all?

You just couldn't leave it be, could you?

If I stand here, unmoving as a monastery, and
you circumscribe me within "your" territory,
will you rename me like that village?

Will you detonate me to shrapnel
because I "stepped out of line"?

Will you wipe me off Earth's face?

Do you remember when your line
disappeared off the jagged road?
You didn't understand.

Earth does not wish to be

drawn upon and quartered.

So where do you draw the line?

SCHRÖDINGER'S ARMENIAN

First published in *HyeBred Magazine*

Homshetsis (Համշէնցիներ; *Hamshentsiner*)
were Western Armenians who migrated
from Urartu to the Black Sea region of
Pontos-Lazona, the soil through which
weave the roots of Lazis, from which
burgeon the stems of *Pontiaká*.

Forgotten people; unspoken tongues.
Fellow West Asians have admitted to
me they've never heard of Laz, nor do
they truly know who Pontians are.

The Tragic Trinity of the Black Sea
formed upon the Homshetsis' arrival.
At least we have each other
to be forgotten with.

Most Homshetsis hardly think themselves "Armenian"
anymore, and opt for *"Hemşinliler"*, not because we
lost our heritage, but because for us in Pontos-Lazona
it was the Qur'ān or the death marches.

And not because we lost our heritage, but
because we sprouted new growth in new
soil—saltier, cooler. Indigenous Laz trickled
into that uprooted Urartian language the way
Tigris flows into Euphrates at al-Qurnah and
became remade, a bloom given new fragrance.

It were the Lazis who helped the Homshetsis
keep living. And the most loving community
I've ever found were the Armenians.

And Homshetsis don't denounce Armenia. *I* don't.
She is to me Մայր Հայաստան (*Mayr Hayastan*)—
Mother Armenia. We emerged from that ancient
lineage—Ani, Sasun, Marash—but one does
not return to the womb that birthed them.

A child is its own entity. One must become
unrecognisable to become Themselves.

"One" is Homshetsi.

Մենք բոլորս Համշենցիներ

(*Menk bolors Hamshentsiner*):

> We are all Homshetsis.

And what if you are wrong?
What if you aren't Homshetsi at all?

Pontic Greeks aren't *Greek* at all, genetically.
DNA is only a thread in the embroidery—
culture is language, custom, socialisation.

And Mother Armenia loves her children.
How many of them was she forced to lay
to rest? How many of them were
cruelly torn from her?

So, say what you will, but whether

Yerevantsi, Artsakhtsi, Sasuntsi,

Myasnikovsky, or Homshetsi,

Mayr Hayastan loves her children.

PIROOZ (پیروز)

for woman (jin/zan), life (jiyan/zendegi), freedom (azadî/âzâdi)

Child of Irân. Son of hope.

Victory didn't die with you.

"CARTOONISH"

I hear it a lot—

"Cartoonish villain".

"Caricature of evil".

Let me tell you of the evils

Reality

has enacted.

Between 1932 and 1972, the US carried out iniquitous

"studies" on the Black men of Tuskegee, Alabama,

"observ[ing] the natural history of untreated syphilis"

in marginalised innocents without the intention to save

them—the coloniser's *pallid[um]* palm saves no one.

They said "6 months".

It became 40 years.

40 years of bismuth, mercury, arsenic.

Poison.

Chemical warfare.

The kicker? Syphilis was treatable by 1947.

Instead, only 74 men remained by the time the nightmare
ended, and 19 babies opened their eyes to a world they'd
never breathe from (*many congenital syphilis deaths
result from lungs drowned in blood*).

> *History* drowns in blood—not the
> cartoonish splatter of strawberry jam, but
> that vile scarlet skag like cut opioids
> pulsing through fleshy veins.

> > > *Real.*

> Flesh and bone, not ink and paper.

Remember "*chemical warfare*"?

Phan Thị Kim Phúc burned in invisible fire rained
from the Vietnamese sky by seppo fighter jets.

Napalm was *real*, visible or not.
To live a life praying for its end;
to hear bombs in fireworks;
to forever see the dying.

We'll *wish* such villainy was merely a cartoon.

When Margaret Atwood spoke of
The Handmaid's Tale, she remarked,
"nothing went into it that had not happened
in real life somewhere at some time."
The blood of West African women stains
every crevice of USA's pallid*[um]* palm.

Every piece of dark fiction a filmmaker has
rendered, Reality has enacted already
and a hundred times worse.

Is *this* the cartoon you speak of?

Maybe I don't see the joke when
I see Êzîdî girls burned alive in
cages by ISIS on my timeline
in Real time instead

(*I haven't slept in 22 years*).

«Чорно́биль» (*Chornóbyl'*) means "black grass"—
Pripyat's water tastes of uranium, still.

Now, tank fuel and ashes.

"Z" is scratched in ugly
Latin script into the walls.
"Z" like Zyklon.
Like irony.

Remember Zyklon?
Napalm's ancestor of chemical warfare?
That was Real too (*the US
education system will
tell you otherwise*).

"Irony" why?

Soviet prisoners of war

were subjected to

human

experimentation

(*remember the evil of Tuskegee?*)

by the Nazis:

Water drenching flesh left to crystallise in subzero
temperature (*that's how the Russians beat Napoleon,
right?*); lungs shrivelling against the touch of hydrogen
cyanide (*how else would they ensure their "Final
Solution" succeeds? [they watch and learn from the
Ottomans]*); streams running red with blood (*I hear
you can still find Dnieper skulls rattling
with bullets in the nearby bogs*).

Mengele, his Death Angel wings blood-caked,
sewed Romani twins together (*I don't need a
flowery metaphor to underscore that evil

                                    Reality*).

Does this villainy still sound "cartoonish"?
Is that harrowing number just "caricature"?

                                    13,000,000

Blackshirts buried *thirteen million* Jews, Roma, Slavs,
queers, yet the US education system allows for
an equal number to deny

                    our Reality.
Such cartoonish villainy can surely not exist!

                    I'll tell you what *did*:

The Red Army's uniform was dyed with blood of
Roma, Jews, queers, Karelians, Kazakhs, Balkars,
Chechens. Even Slavs.

> *Is this evil Real yet?*

Stalin razed the very Caucasus that birthed him, now
he's buried in the Kremlin (*you don't deserve to return*
to the sacred womb of Kavkasia's burnt body—burnt
like Phan Thị Kim Phúc; burnt like the Êzidî girls).

100 days of slaughter (*1994*) wiped nearly
a million Tutsi off Rwanda's scarred face.
2 million Rwandan citizens—Hutu, Tutsi,
Twa—fled, only now beginning to return
like water to a drained dam (*it's 2020s as I write*).

> *2,000,000*

Some 2 million indigenous corpses (*1915*)
lie beneath the glitzy hotels
of Türkiye's resorts.

> 412 million bones.

> *I want the bones of my patrída back.*

They are Real and I can feel them

beneath the parquet as I walk.

They will

never return.

People like to ask me what I

am, so I will ask *you* what

a cartoon is *not*.

hint:

Real.

What kind of man gleefully begets

the murder of *1, 2, 13* million?

What kind of man watches hundreds

of innocents succumb to

preventable illness?

What kind of man stitches two beings into one?

What kind of man burns

alive his own Mother?

What kind of man?

A *real* one.

Not a cartoon.

Not caricature.

A *man.*

A human.
An idea.
Dogma.
A book.
Theology.

Propaganda.
Think of the children!

Ignorance.
Hate.
Fear.
Corruption.

Reality.

Cartoons and caricature will
always be safe abstractions.

Reality has enacted
the darkest evils
already

and a hundred times worse.

DARK ONLY DARK

Dark daughter, *dark* daylight,

Karanlık *kız*, karanlık *gün ışığı*,

dead *body*, everlastingly *foreign.*

ceset, *ebediyen* ecnebi.

I'D DO ANYTHING
FOR ABATEMENT

I've bitten deep enough to

rip the skin off my own arm

from the unbearable weight of this blood

but it didn't lighten the load.

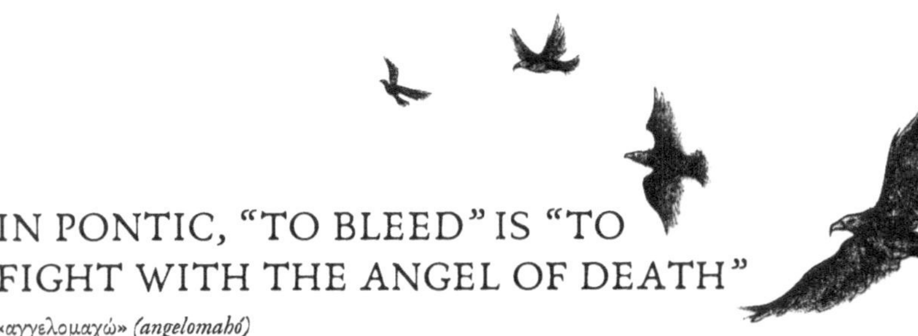

IN PONTIC, "TO BLEED" IS "TO FIGHT WITH THE ANGEL OF DEATH"

«αγγελομαχώ» *(angelomahó)*

First published in *Our Ghazal* by *Qafiyah Review* under *Bleed I and Bleed We*

Wounds: a gateway carved into my flesh,

my roots, my *patrída*'s bones.

          "*Kılıç artıkları!*" they sneer.

"*Leftovers of the sword*": roots remaining

in an earth blood-watered.

Soumelá grieves for recollective silence;

if you chip off a piece, it tastes of

antídoron and defiled marrow.

When astrocytes scar it's gliosis;

when the mind scars it's heartache.

«Εγώ Ποντιόπουλ' είμαι· ματώνω κι ματούμαι.»

    (*Eḡó Pontiópoul' íme; matóno ki matoúme.*)

        "*Pontian, I am;*

        bleed I and bleed we."

The gateway into my flesh still parts where veins twist
like roots in cyanotic syncope—so oft-traversed its
scarred agape to bare my patrída's bones:
antídoron for the desert-walkers.

Cut-up *Borçx̱a* (ბორჩხა) heals to *Borçk̲a* (…)

Our mountains of karst lapped by the black seas still
seep a gunky red—unwashable—like the last
Caspian tiger comforting his own loneliness.

Şeçeri desert sand crunches beneath my bleeding
feet as I trail my father's unspooled brains

          back home.

Ottoman leftovers behind a *yaşmak*
—stretched over
bone-baring wounds.

My wounds: a gateway;

a bottomless cavern I walk

through before day breaks and

when night falls, tracing its

tattered ridges

like scars.

My tattered ridges.

My scars.

Rough as mountains of

karst, as black seas, as

recollective silence.

THE RIVER (*English*)

Red river, red river;

      redhead river.

She has no name.

    She says, "*I make widows*".

      Bones on the riverbed—bones of my homeland.

I speak of it ceaselessly.

        "*You exist because of us!*"

    Thus…

Red hair on my brow—

      soaked with dye.

        Blood.

  I   into the river
   fall   to cleanse myself.

        To find Gnosis.

   Apokatastasis.

Red blood unto red river—

    my blood makes

      a redhead river.

  Redhead river makes me

    a brunette

    (*again*).

Red river,
red river.
She has no name.

ΤΟ ΠΟΤΆΜΙ (*Greek*)

Κόκκινο ποτάμι, κόκκινο ποτάμι·
Kókkino potámi, kókkino potámi;

κοκκινομάλλα ποτάμι.
kokkinomálla potámi.

Αυτή δεν έχει όνομα.
Aftí den éhi ónoma.

Αυτή λέγει, «δημιουργώ χήρες».
Aftí léγi, "dimiurğó híres".

Οστά επί του ποταμού κοίτη—οστά της πατρίδα μου.
Ostá epí tou potamoú koíti—ostá tis patríḍa mou.

Ομιλώ ατέλειωτα γι' αυτό.
Omiló atéleota γi' aftó.

«Υπάρχεις λόγω εμάς!»
"Ypárhes lóğo emás!"

Ούτως...
Útos...

Κόκκινα μαλλιά επί μετώπου εμένα—
Kókkina malliá epí metópou eména—

εμποτισμένα με βαφή.
ebotisména me vafí.

Αίμα.
Aíma.

Εγώ   στο ποτάμι
Eğó   *sto potámi*

για να εξαγνίζω ο εαυτός μου.
γia na exağnízo o eaftós mou.

πέφτω
péfto

Για να έβρω Γνῶσις.
γia na évro Ğnôsis.

Ἀποκατάστᾰσις.
Apokatástasis.

Κόκκινο αίμα προς κόκκινο ποτάμι—
Kókkino aíma pros kókkino potámi—

το αίμα μου δημιουργεί ενα κοκκινομάλλα ποτάμι.
to aíma mou ḍimiurğí ena kokkinomálla potámi.

Κοκκινομάλλα ποτάμι
Kokkinomálla potámi.

με μετατρέπει σε μελαχρινή
me metatrépi se melahriní

(ξανά).
(xaná).

Κόκκινο ποτάμι,
Kókkino potámi,

κόκκινο ποτάμι.
kókkino potámi.

Αυτή δεν έχει όνομα.
Aftí den éhi ónoma.

SPOILS OF FAMINE

First published in *The Globe Review*

If humanity is a rye field, then hunger is a scythe blow; coarse cold karst grinding between itself seed to flour.

Flour to water to salt to softness kneaded between a daughter's diligent fingers. The softness clings to the bosom of a *satz'* (pan) like the neighbours' bairn to its mother, ripens to the ashy crust of bread like a worker's calluses. *Perék* is to be shared, this side of the Black Sea (we call it *Eúxinos Póntos* [Εύξεινος Πόντος]— "Hospitable Sea", or simply *Uça Zuğa* [უჩა ზუღა]— "Black Sea").

Perék fills the gnawing gut of the old father and his daughter, her worker husband, their neighbours, to dilute its provincial sourness, so humanity may be impelled by hunger anew.

Famine soon rakes the ragged Laz terrains.
Scythe has no more rye to cut, karst has no more seed to grind to flour, so the scythe turns on the body, and the body turns to the karst—a starved corpse eaten by the mountains who beg to live no quieter than the neighbours' bairn.

The worker—the daughter's husband—drops in the rye field. The daughter weeps for the stillness in his ribs and the bread she won't knead. Her fingers are stiff with hunger.

The neighbour with her bairn stands at the door. "*Sýzygos mou* (my spouse) and I gleaned of your tragedy." Her slumberless voice suggests a bid at radiance—poor things have slept not a blink from hunger for weeks. "Before it is usurped by the overflowing fat of Ottomans, I bring a meagre gift; indebtedness for your *perék* and *anarántzin* (bitter orange)." She hands the daughter a pouch of flour, dainty as a heart.

The daughter collapses at the neighbour's feet and weeps and weeps in gratitude.

The old father watches on, black eyes burning upon the pouch dangling from his daughter's fist.

See, hunger is a scythe blow to humanity, and desperation can grind away man's dignity (*can one lay blame upon such corollary?*)

The daughter puts flour to water to salt to softness kneaded between her diligent fingers. The softness clings to the bosom of a *satz'*, ripens to the ashy crust of bread, small as the neighbour's kind act, yet worth in equal.

The old father watches covetously.

The daughter feels his gaze, comprehends the burn behind it. She cuts the bread to eleven pieces—the number of Türkiye's provinces constituting historic Pontos/ Lazona—and brings them to her gracious neighbours; the Lazis across the path; the Homshetsis higher up the hills; even the skinny grimalkin walking her own yard (the creature refuses the meatlessness of it). The daughter, too, slips a piece into her own *fóta* (apron).

The final piece, the daughter brings to her old father, lays it in his palm and closes his frozen fingers around it, kissing his brow, and the man weeps and weeps in gratitude, repentance, grasping the error of his greedy ways.

And so it stands that every trait dubbed "feminine" is done so in bad faith. For nurturing, care, love... Are those not merely *human* traits? And what is a human stripped of sensitivities for suffering?

Hunger is, in chorus, a scythe blow tearing away the flimsy veil of self-grandeur; coarse cold karst grinding away prickly complexes of superiority.

Hunger is humanity's soberest impetus.

WE ARE OUR EARTH

for Lazona

ვოი (*voi*), ვოი, ვოი.

    Lament of wind and karst; soughing branches becoming
    dendrites and lungs—flesh of earth; earth is flesh. *Vein-root.*
    Even the ink-Black Sea scribes its tale of
    far-off journeys upon the parchment shore.
    The land telling vetust stories to its child.

ვოი, ვოი.

    Who remains to listen?
    Child in exile; torn from the bosom of karst.
    Her own child torn in turn. Branchless trees;
    veins uprooted. Earth twice-barren.
    The Sea chews the marrow of the exiled,
    starved of stories to tell. *Only laments.*

A birthmark is a storyteller's inkblot.
So we sink to the parchment shore
to drink the Sea. To *reroot veins*
in amnestic flesh.

To remember how to tell our tales again.

I'VE DREAMED

I've dreamed of seeing the Old City.

Walled. Preserved. A time capsule. A crucible.

I've dreamed of seeing the Christian Quarter at
midnight.

Where the *Church of the Anastasis* holds its
deepnight vigil with its bricks of *prósphora* and
the eclipsed moon red as Yēshūa's blood overhead.
Many years ago already I deconverted, but still some
nights I whisper that ghostly moniker, *O Naós tis
Anastáseos tou Kyríou*, and I cross myself, and
I dream of seeing the Christian Quarter.

I've dreamed of seeing the Armenian Quarter at
eventide.

To drink *soorj* at the bookshop near *Gulbenkian
Library*. To breathe in the tangerines and
mu'assel as clouds bloom to lilac bouquets.
To dream of a liberated Hayastan.

I've dreamed of seeing the HaKótel at noon.

> Beneath the blazing sun of Canaan.
> I'll watch from afar, not intruding.
> I'll watch from afar, and retreat to the
> olive-grove shade from the sun's nip
> across my nose—such a simple thing.
> I dream of simple things.

I've dreamed of seeing the Muslim Quarter at dawn.

> As *Sūq al-Qaṭṭānīn* begins to languidly
> rouse, and sunblinks skim the gilden
> *Dome*, and I dream of blinding
> the close-circuit cameras.

I've dreamed of seeing the Moroccan Quarter rebuilt.

> Founded by a child of Kurds.
> I dream of an untouched
> *Bou Medyan* zaouïa.

I dream of seeing the Old City.

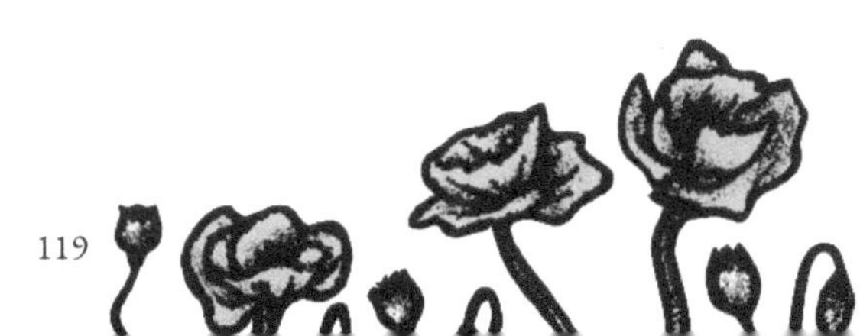

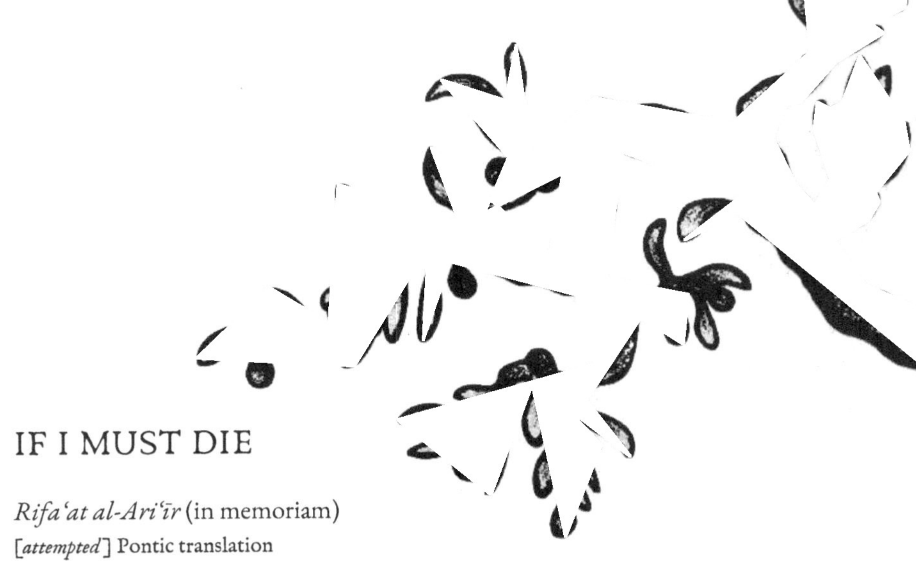

IF I MUST DIE

Rifa'at al-Ari'īr (in memoriam)
[*attempted*] Pontic translation

ΑΝ ΠΡΆΤΤΩ ΑΧΆΤΕ ΑΠΟΨΥΧΊΖΩ

Ριφα ἀτ αλ-Αρι ἵρ (εις μνήμην)

[*ανεπιτυχής*] Ποντιακή μετάφραση

Αν πράττω αχάτε αποψυχίζω,
An prátto aháte apopsyhízo,

εσύ πράττεις αχάτε ζήσεις
esý práttis aháte zísis

γιανά πεις τ' στορέα μου,
yianá pis t' storéa mou,

γιανά πούλησες τ' πράγματά μου,
yianá poúlises t' prâḡmatá mou,

γιανά αγοράζεις ένα πανίν
yianá aḡorázis éna panín

κι ένα κλωστάριν,
ki éna klostárin,

(ευτάγε το λευκό με μακρόσυρτο κατούρεμαν)
(eftáye to lefkó me makrósyrto katoúreman)

γιανά πορεί ένα γαρδέλι, κάπερου στην Γάζα,
yianá porí éna ḡarḏéli, káperou stin Ḡáza,

όντες αντικρύζεις τον ουρανό στα ομμάτοπα,
óntes antikrýzis ton ouranó sta ommátora,

120

αναμένοντας τον πατέρα του
anaménontas ton patéra tou

νέρ᾽ έφυγε σαν μια βρούλα—
nér' éfyye san mia vroúla—

κι δεν αποχαιρέτησε κάνα,
ki den apoherétise kána,

νέ καν τον σόιν του,
né kan ton sóin tou,

νέ καν κιαντή—
né kan kiantí—

να ελέπει την πεταλήτρα, την πεταλήτρα
na elépi tin petalítra, tin petalítra

μου νέρ᾽ έκαμες· φτεράκισμει άνθεν,
mou nér' ékames; fterákismi ánthen,

κι για μια στιγμή θαρεί πως ακεί
ki yia mia stiğmí tharí pos akí

είναι ένας άγγελος—φέροντας
íne énas ángelos—férontas

πίσω Αγάπεμαν.
píso Ağápeman.

Αν πράττω αχάτε αποψυχίζω,
An prátto aháte apopsyhízo,

ας φέρει θάρρεμαν.
as féri thárreman.

Ας γίνει μασάλιν.
As yíni masálin.

A FINAL INCANTATION

Please.

Give us hope.

Let *justice* prevail somewhere in this world.

Give us hope.

Give us hope.

Give us hope.

fin...

your Goodreads and
StoryGraph reviews &
ratings are appreciated

Acknowledgements

First of all, I would like to extend the utmost gratitude to the leftist, queer, minority SWANA community I have both found and cultivated online, not least of whom include Sophia, Ayşe-Mira, Sila, Lilly, Nicole, Leila, Zanshawa, Arev, ميناس (*Minnie*), and Milan among so many more. Your presence is so sacred, I don't think I have ever found a circle more accepting, something which has made reconnection with my SWANA roots so much easier. I'm forever indebted.

I doubt I'd be writing poetry at all if it weren't for my most beloved poets, most notably Maḥmūd Darwīsh, Noor Hindi, Moḥammed El-Kurd, Audre Lorde, Moṣab Abū Toha, Daniel Barzilay, Minney Richani, and, of course, Traci Brimhall. Every single piece written by these people means the universe to me.

Thanks must extend also to the literary magazines which have accepted my work prior to its publication as an anthology here, most of all Agavny Vardanyan, curator of the *Split Pomegranate* charity zine for Artsakh. Մերսի, ջան.

დიდი მადლობა.

Ուղիկ' էրիի.

Благодарю вас.

Φχαριστώ τελα.

Sag boluň.

کنم از شما تشکر می

Thank you.

~Sfar

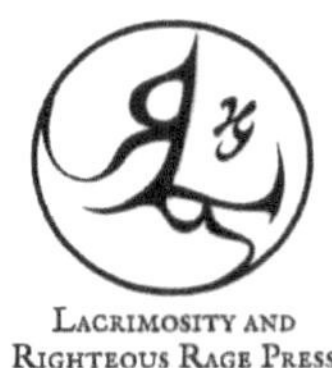

Lacrimosity and
Righteous Rage Press